"... so I went, laden with charges from my mother to walk in the middle of the street (they jump out on you as you are turning a corner), never to venture forth after sunset, and always to lock up everything (I who could never lock up anything, except my heart in company)."

So states James Matthew Barrie (1860–1937), describing his first venture into London in 1885. This confession provides a clue to the writer's character—at once a revealing author, and a man who maintained an emotional distance from his admiring readers.

MY HEART IN COMPANY

The Work of J. M. Barrie and the Birth of Peter Pan

TIMOTHY G. YOUNG

Beinecke Rare Book and Manuscript Library

Yale University, New Haven, Connecticut

Distributed by University Press of New England

February 3 through April 23, 2005
Beinecke Rare Book and Manuscript Library
Yale University, New Haven, Connecticut

COVER IMAGE:
"There now arose a mighty storm and he was tossed this way and that."
Original illustration by Arthur Rackham from *Peter Pan in Kensington Gardens,*
ca. 1905, pen, ink, and watercolor

DEDICATION

THE COLLECTIONS IN THE Beinecke Rare Book and Manuscript Library were formed through the dedication of librarians and donors who shared a wide range of interests that all related to books and reading. While Walter Beinecke, one of the three brothers who endowed the library's construction, was not a book collector himself, his children shared the passions of his two brothers who were. Walter Beinecke, Jr. (known to everyone as Bud), found a healthy obsession with all things related to J. M. Barrie, as his uncle E. J. had with his lifelong collecting of Robert Louis Stevenson. Bud Beinecke bought Barrie books and manuscripts when Barrie was not much in vogue. He successfully acquired much of the collection of Cynthia Asquith, Barrie's secretary in his later years, as well as key items from a variety of other sources. His Barrie collection, presented to the library beginning in the early 1960s, complemented a core collection of books given by Yale alumnus Henry C. Taylor in 1948, making Yale a required stop for anyone writing about Barrie.

Bud's sister, Betsy Beinecke Shirley, found her own interest in the broad tradition of American children's literature and spent many years building a representative collection of the most important editions from the past 300 years.

Bud Beinecke passed away at the age of 86 in May 2004. His sister, Betsy, died three months later at the age of 84. In honor of their devotion to books, to the library, and to their own passions for the many ways childhood has been celebrated, we dedicate this exhibition.

This catalogue focuses on highlights from the exhibition, *My Heart in Company: The Work of J. M. Barrie and the Birth of Peter Pan*, on view at the Beinecke Library from February 3 through April 23, 2005. Iconic objects have been chosen to form a timeline that traces the development of Barrie's work in connection with his life. Several books, many of which served as useful references for this exhibition, offer more complete accounts of Barrie's life. Among these are:

Andrew Birkin, *J. M. Barrie & the Lost Boys,* new ed. (New Haven: Yale University Press, 2003).

Janet Dunbar, *J. M. Barrie: The Man Behind the Image* (London: Collins, 1970).

Denis George Mackail, *Barrie; The Story of J. M. B.* (New York: Charles Scribner's Sons, 1941).

MY HEART IN COMPANY

Timothy G. Young

HOW SHOULD WE TALK ABOUT J. M. BARRIE? One hundred years after the premiere of his most famous creation, *Peter Pan* (for most audiences his only famous invention), he remains an obscure figure. The majority of his works are little known, even to students of late Victorian era British literature, and his life, read principally in connection to *Peter Pan,* is a conjectural mixture of uncomfortable obsessions and loosely interpreted personal statements. Barrie deserves a close reappraisal, not only because he was one of the most widely read popular writers of his era—both in England and in America—but also owing to the fascinating evolution of themes of his later works, when he surmounted the sentimental, turning from a Victorian youth into an Edwardian man.

Barrie was a good example of the type of writer against whom proper Modernists would rebel. Though he held an emotional place in the hearts of many 20th-century writers, as a rule, his quaint-seeming, nostalgic subject matter and his emotionally manipulative style would have been anathema to someone like Virginia or Leonard Woolf, whose animosity toward Robert Louis Stevenson, a close friend of Barrie and like-minded writer, has been noted (Leonard Woolf, "The Fall of Stevenson," in *Essays on Literature, History, Politics etc.* [London: Hogarth Press, 1927]).

Barrie serves as an upstanding example of a late-19th-century success story. Coming from a very modest background in a small Scottish town, he successfully made himself through education, reading, and writing. Precociously productive, writing regular book reviews for the Edinburgh *Evening Courant* while still in college, he knew that he would be an author from an early age. His foray into London in 1885 at age 24, where he was famously met by a newsstand displaying a copy of the *St. James's Gazette* featuring an article he had submitted, was like a chapter from a novel. Next came the nervous meeting with the editor, a tentative presentation of stories, and the confirmation that more work would be accepted. The type of work that the editor, Frederick Greenwood, requested would have a significant impact on the direction that Barrie pursued as a writer.

The stories that proved most popular were Barrie's fictionalized tales of his childhood village. Thus, Barrie found himself in the interstice between journalism and fiction, writing to inform and to please popular tastes. His writing for the next decade followed this pattern. Far from being a fantasist, Barrie played to the pull of his appreciative audience. After his first play, a treatment of the life of Richard Savage, failed, he quickly produced a follow-up, at the beckoning of the popular stage comedian J. L. Toole, a parody of *Hedda Gabler*. Its success reinforced the direction of his work—popular subjects begetting wide reaction.

Through the 1890s, as he became more widely read on both sides of the Atlantic, his subject matter, in his novels, essays, and plays, addressed gentle subjects that still fill light fiction today: the foibles of men and their manners (*Walker, London*), tobacco and other diversions in a bachelor's life (*My Lady Nicotine*), further stories of small-town characters (*The Little Minister*). The apex of this era of his writing can be seen in *Sentimental Tommy,* the novel that combined his deepest autobiographical motifs with his emotionally laden narrative style. The story of Tommy Sandys's life hews very closely to a modern soap opera with its recurrent threats to any type of true happiness in the life of a central character who is ultimately unknowable.

The years during which Barrie created his fully formed literary analogue, 1894 and 1895, were filled with events that pushed him toward a fuller maturity: his marriage to Mary Ansell, the loss of his friend and erstwhile mentor, Robert Louis Stevenson, and the death of his mother, Margaret Ogilvy. The following years saw a shift in his writing that would come to flower after the turn of the century. It can be observed that Barrie's growth away from sentimentality was marked cleanly around 1900 as he was finishing revisions to *Tommy and Grizel,* the sequel to *Sentimental Tommy,* just as he was making notes for a fairy story centering around a sprite who inhabited Kensington Gardens. As he killed off Tommy Sandys, he gave birth to Peter Pan.

In the new century, Barrie continued to produce crowd-pleasing farces and comedies, such as *Quality Street,* but other plays introduced far-reaching social commentary, as in *The Admirable Crichton,* a popular play that explored the effects of reversals in social hierarchy. Barrie mainly dedicated himself to the stage after 1902, issuing only short prose pieces, such as essays and speeches on his own work and on fellow writers. He addressed war themes during the First World War, as well as drawing on Shakespeare to examine the possibility of living life over without regrets (*Dear Brutus*). The magic wood in that play functions much like the desert island in *The Admirable Crichton* — both are realms of displacement wherein Barrie's characters are freed of restraint to explore the limits of fantasy — much like his best-known dreamworld: Never Land.

If Barrie is hidden in the shadows, Peter Pan must be the most public of characters. No mention of children's theater post-1904 can ring without the sound of that ticking clock or those fairy bells. Yet, a survey asking well-read adults who created Peter Pan might elicit reactions that the story of Peter just simply exists — like a myth or folktale. Peter Pan is around us every day: he is a brand of peanut butter, a line of top-selling women's bras, the ubiquitous bus company that crisscrosses New England. Is it possible to reconnect Peter to his origins? It is fair enough to let him go, to exist as a touchstone, reimagined by Hollywood, Broadway, and Disney, but there is a genesis that must be acknowledged.

Peter sprang from the imagination of James Matthew Barrie — one fueled by a childhood love of adventure stories (including plenty of pirates), the Victorian vogue for fairies, and his mythologizing the landmarks of Kensington Gardens for the amusement of the Llewelyn Davies brothers. It is certain that these five brothers were at the heart of the story, as lovingly explained by Barrie in his 1928 dedication to the text of the *Peter Pan* play. They gave off the spark, but Barrie was the craftsman who tended the flame.

To reclaim Peter as Barrie's creation, one has to find him as he first appeared in *The Little White Bird,* the book that revolved around his tale-telling to George and Jack Llewelyn Davies in the early days of their friendship. Peter Pan is first mentioned in Chapter 13, prior to his proper introduction in the following chapter, as a half-human baby riding in a thrush's nest across the Serpentine in Kensington Gardens. He is described with certain characteristics of his mythological namesake, Pan, as a curious, pipe-playing liaison between humans and fairies.

Barrie's storytelling about Peter diverges into two paths — the storybook Peter and the stage Peter. In *The Little White Bird,* and in the later expansion of the Peter Pan chapters (as *Peter Pan in Kensington Gardens*), Peter makes the acquaintance of a little human girl,

Maimie Mannering, who teases him with a kiss, a sequence that hews closely to the flirtation of Peter and Wendy in the stage play, but the infant Peter has a distinctly more disturbing mission in Kensington Gardens. While the stage Peter exists for pleasure ("Fun is all Peter wants" Barrie wrote in his notes), the storybook baby Peter's tasks include burying the bodies of dead children who have fallen out of their perambulators.

The stage version of *Peter Pan* proved so popular that this Peter—as a boy who didn't want to grow up, who gathered (living) lost children around him (boys only, as girls were too smart to leave home)—became iconic. Curiously, though a few storybooks tied to the play were issued in the wake of its success, the storybook version Barrie offered to the reading public was the tale of the baby Peter. Only in 1911, seven years after the first performance of the play and following a consistent run of revivals, did Barrie offer a narrative version of the play in *Peter and Wendy*. This is the book version that is most often found in bookstores today under the simplified title *Peter Pan*. The text of the play was not published until 1928, by which time it seemed as though the story had entered the universal subconscious of all English-born children.

If J. M. Barrie is not accorded his due in a critical overview of English literature, this may be because his biography looms much larger than the body of his work. The relationship of Barrie to his young friends, later his wards, the Llewelyn Davies brothers, is the lens through which he is discussed today. This story has been written about, analyzed, and filmed, at least twice, in an attempt to both get at the heart of Peter Pan and to explain, for its own sake, the depth of Barrie's dedication to a family of children who were not his own flesh and blood.

Barrie's focus on the nature of childhood seen in his early works, especially the Auld Licht essays, which communicate a simple, but rather unbothered playful youth, grew stronger when he became an uncle. In "Peterkin: A Marvel of Nature," published in the Edinburgh *Evening Dispatch* in 1889, Barrie rhapsodized about his rough and tumble play with his nephew Charlie. He also doted on little Margaret Henley and Bevil Quiller-Couch before he met George and Jack and Peter Llewelyn Davies.

The question that lurks in much of the biographical research and analysis of Barrie centers on the extent and nature of his obsession with the Llewelyn Davies brothers.

Though the photographs of the boys playing in *The Boy Castaways of Black Lake Island* include a couple of them splashing around nude in the lake, Barrie does not appear to have been erotically charged as Lewis Carroll was in his photography of his own fixation, Alice Liddell. One must also figure into the discussion Barrie's lifelong pattern of powerful crushes on beautiful leading ladies, one of whom he married.

The fact that Barrie's marriage ended in divorce, precipitated by infidelity (not his), complicates the discussion of his later life. The odd twist of fate that made him guardian to the Llewelyn Davies brothers, moving him from an avuncular to a paternal role, made his life story more dramatic than anything he could have written in his early career.

Such details are what will continue to fuel examinations of Barrie's life, in many ways to the detriment of the study of his work. On looking at the list of Barrie's publications in print in 2004, after sorting out the many editions of *Peter Pan*, it is reassuring to see that many of his plays and best-known novels are still available. Whether *The Little Minister* will be read for pleasure or for a taste of Victorian treacle is up to the individual reader.

The beauty of a library dedicated to the preservation of a bibliographically complete set of printed works and a complex manuscript collection is the freedom to study and work out new interpretations of the work and the writer's biography. This exhibition aims to show some of the key pieces in the Beinecke's collections that inform our understanding of J. M. Barrie. The title for the exhibition, *My Heart in Company,* is deliberately ambivalent, as drawn directly from Barrie's own writing. In a chapter of *Margaret Ogilvy,* the biography he wrote of his mother, Barrie described his first trip to London, noting: ". . . so I went, laden with charges from my mother to walk in the middle of the street (they jump out on you as you are turning a corner), never to venture forth after sunset, and always to lock up everything (I who could never lock up anything, except my heart in company)." In this innocent recollection, he posits his mystery for us. Though he lived a very public life and based much of his writing on his own experiences, he kept his secrets closely guarded. It is up to us, his readers, to come to our own decision about his reasons for doing so.

*The Work of J. M. Barrie
and the Birth of Peter Pan*

Amateur Dramatic Club.

MEMBERS.

Mr W. ANDERSON.

Mr J. BARRIE.

Mr L. BENNETT.

Mr J. BLACKLOCK.

Mr H. GRIEVE.

Mr H. M'EWEN.

Mr T. NEWBIGGING.

Mr G. SMITH.

Mr J. SMITH.

Secretary, … … … …	Mr J. BARRIE.
Acting Manager, … …	Mr W. ANDERSON.
Stage Manager, … … …	Mr J. SMITH.

Applications for Seats and other Enquiries to be made to the Managers.

PROGRAMME.

To commence this Evening with the *successful* Comedy-Drama entitled

OFF THE LINE !

Harry Coke, an Engine-driver, … … …	Mr J. BARRIE.
Jim Brass, his Stoker, … … …	Mr L. BENNETT
Lizzie Coke, Harry's wife, … …	Mr W. ANDERSON
Mary Coke, Harry's sister, … … …	Mr H. M'EWEN
Puffy, in love with Mary, … … …	Mr G. SMITH

To be followed by *Le Petit Drame Sensational*, in Six Tableaux, entitled

BANDELERO, THE BANDIT.

Bandelero, … … … … …	Mr T. NEWBIGGING
Sir Richard Vernon, … …	Mr H. GRIEVE
Alice, his daughter, … … …	Mr H. M'EWEN
Smike, … … *(his original character)*	Mr J. BARRIE
Gamp, … … … } Villains { …	Mr L. BENNETT
Benshaw, … … }	Mr J. BLACKLOCK
Father Dolan, a priest, … … …	Mr G. SMITH

To conclude with a Laughable Comedietta, in Two Acts, taken from the favourite Comedy of

PAUL PRY.

Major-General Johnston, … … …	Mr T. NEWBIGGING
Phœbe, his daughter, … … …	Mr J. BARRIE
Old Witherton, … … … …	Mr J. BLACKLOCK
Mrs Briggs, housekeeper to Witherton, …	Mr G. SMITH
Paul Pry, … … … …	Mr W. ANDERSON
Frank, Witherton's nephew, home from abroad,…	Mr H. GRIEVE
Simon, Briggs' confidential servant, … …	Mr J. SMITH
Doubledot, innkeeper, … … …	Mr L. BENNETT

1877 *Playbill for* BANDELERO THE BANDIT

J. M. BARRIE'S CHILDHOOD was filled with the expected Victorian boyish pursuits. Growing up in a family of modest means in Kirriemuir, Scotland, he found pleasure in inexpensive editions of authors such as Sir Walter Scott, Thomas Mayne Reid, and R. M. Ballantyne, as well as serialized adventures in "penny dreadfuls," brightly colored cheap booklets that nearly every young boy bought and traded. These tales filtered into Barrie's first attempts at writing.

In 1873, at the age of 13, Barrie moved to the household of his oldest brother Alexander, who was serving as the Inspector of Schools for the district of Dumfries. Barrie entered Dumfries Academy, where he made friends with other precocious readers, a group of students who formed the Dumfries Amateur Dramatic Club. The first season saw the production of Barrie's *Bandelero the Bandit*. An energetic cobbling together of outlaw themes Barrie had been reading, it was based mainly on tales of James Fennimore Cooper, another of his favorite authors.

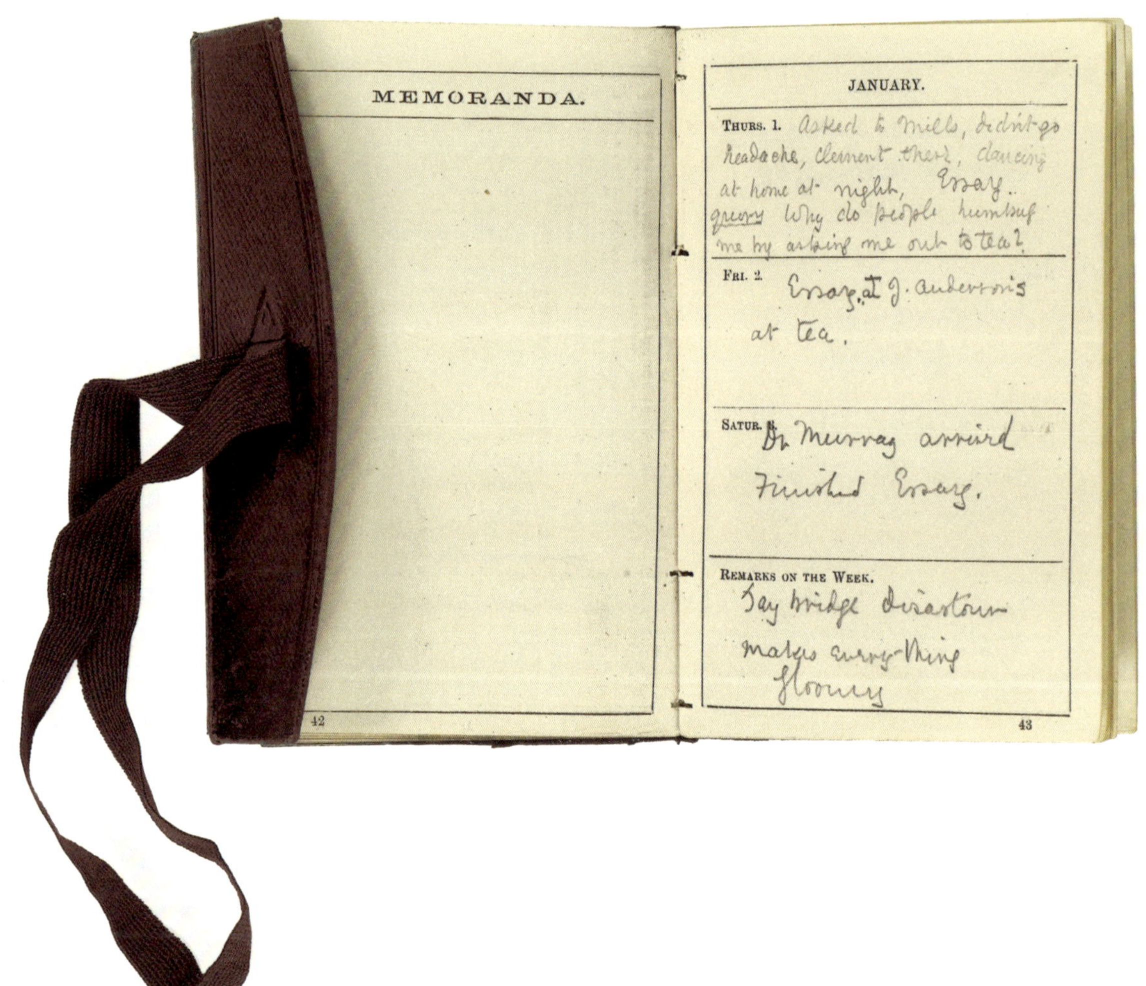

MEMORANDA.

JANUARY.

THURS. 1. Asked to Mills, didn't go
headache, Clement there, dancing
at home at night, Essay..
query Why do people humbug
me by asking me out to tea?

FRI. 2. Essay at J. Anderson's
at tea.

SATUR. 3. Dr Murray arrived
Finished Essay.

REMARKS ON THE WEEK.
Tay bridge disaster
makes everything
gloomy

1880 *Diary*

In January 1880, J. M. Barrie was 19 years old and in the middle of his second year at Edinburgh University. Though busy with his studies, he was already reviewing books on a regular basis for the Edinburgh *Evening Courant* and had begun contributing drama criticism. This, his "Campbell's Victorian Diary and Almanac for 1880," is one of the few diaries Barrie kept. He begins the new year by noting his inability to visit a friend "Mills" (possibly a bookseller in Kirriemuir) and by complaining, "Why do people humbug me by asking me out to tea?" The diary continues with notations of visits with friends, dates for theater-going, exams, and, quite often, the repeated assessment of many things, "Humbug!"

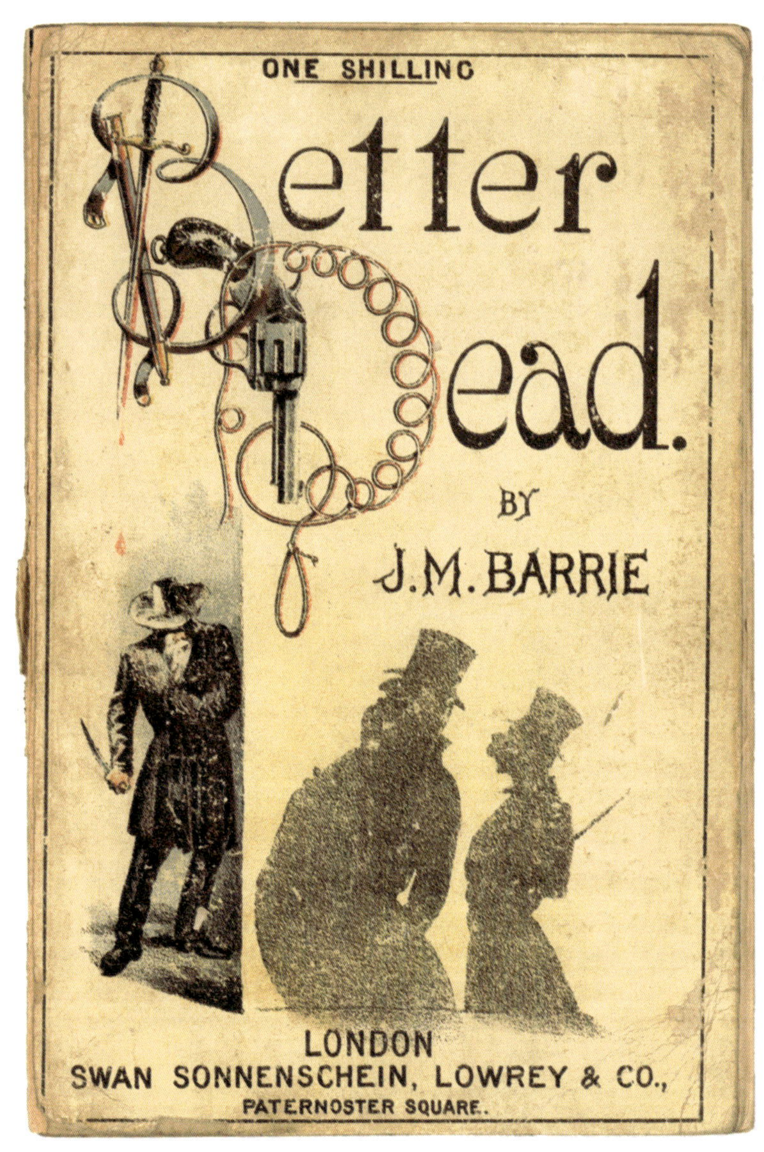

ONE SHILLING
Better Dead.
BY
J.M. BARRIE
LONDON
SWAN SONNENSCHEIN, LOWREY & CO.,
PATERNOSTER SQUARE.

1887 BETTER DEAD

IN 1885, BARRIE MOVED TO LONDON, girded with cautionary advice from his mother, and set forth to find the best outlet for his writing. Upon arriving, he discovered that an article he had submitted to Frederick Greenwood, editor of the *St. James's Gazette,* was on the newsstand. Barrie pursued this relationship with increasing success over the next several years.

One of the first articles Greenwood accepted from Barrie in London had a strange premise, a fantasy about the "Society for Doing Without Some People"—simply put, a scheme for removing annoying public figures and, thus, freeing up newspaper column inches for more deserving news. The story was eventually expanded to novel length and published, as *Better Dead,* at the author's expense, at the end of 1887. It was Barrie's first separate publication bearing his name.

CHAPTER II.

THRUMS.

THRUMS is the name I give here to the handful of houses jumbled together in a cup, which is the town nearest the school-house. Until twenty years ago its every other room, earthen-floored and showing the rafters overhead, had a handloom, and hundreds of weavers lived and died Thoreaus "ben the hoose" without knowing it. In those days the cup overflowed and left several houses on the top of the hill, where their cold skeletons still stand. The road that climbs from the square, which is Thrums's heart, to the north is so steep and straight, that in a sharp frost children hunker at the top and are blown down with

1888 *Page from* AULD LICHT IDYLLS

BARRIE'S FIRST WAVE of widespread fame came upon the publication of *Auld Licht Idylls* in 1888, a collection of articles based on life in his childhood village, Kirriemuir. These fictionalized memoirs treated small town life in Scotland in the 19th century with an intense nostalgic sentimentality and a precious use of dialect—elements that mark what has come to be known as "the Kailyard School" (from the Scottish for "kitchen garden"), as exemplified by writers Ian MacLaren and S. R. Crockett.

The Auld Licht community in "Thrums" that Barrie wrote about was a 19th-century remnant of a conservative, even puritanical, sect of the Church of Scotland, that had seceded in the 18th century. Robert Burns wrote about the sect, whose name means "Old Light," in his poem "The Ordination." Barrie's mother, Margaret Ogilvy, had been raised in the Auld Licht church but later changed to the Free Church of her husband, David Barrie, though she apparently retained many of her Auld Licht ways.

The last line on the page concludes: " . . . a roar and a rush on rails of ice."

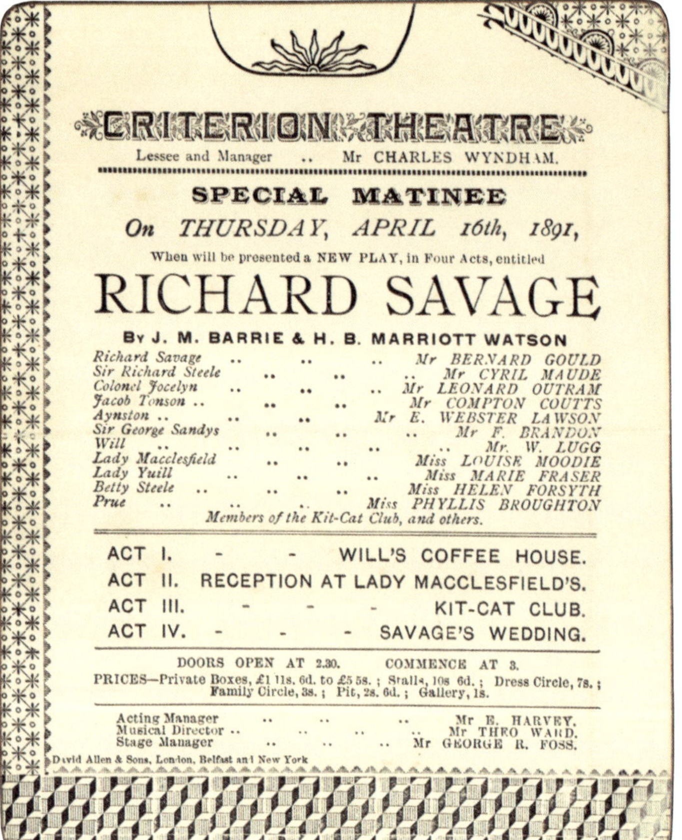

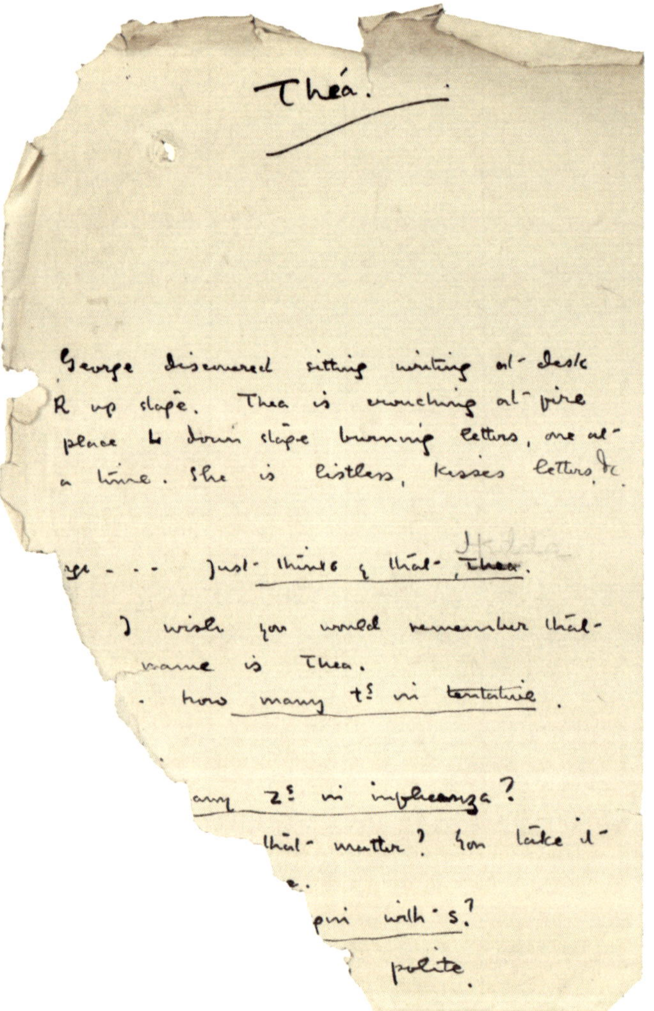

Théa.

George discovered sitting writing at desk
R up stage. Thea is crouching at fire-
place L down stage burning letters, one at
a time. She is listless, kisses letters &c

...ge ... Just think of that, Thea.

I wish you would remember that
name is Thea.
. how many t's in tentative .

...any z's in influenza?
...that matter? You take it
...
...pin with s?
...polite.

1891 *Playbill for* RICHARD SAVAGE

and draft page from IBSEN'S GHOST

BARRIE'S FIRST ADULT PLAY that he saw produced was *Richard Savage,* a drama based on the life of the eponymous poet, a friend of Dr. Samuel Johnson. The play, done in collaboration with his fellow journalist, the New Zealand-born H. B. Marriott Watson, had a single performance in April 1891.

Barrie soon turned his attention to another project that would prove much more rewarding. For the famous comic actor J. L. Toole, he crafted a burlesque based on *Hedda Gabler. Ibsen's Ghost,* which was originally titled *Thea,* premiered in May of 1891, to resounding laughter and applause. J. L. Toole went on to star in Barrie's next stage success, *Walker, London* in 1892.

Garrick Club
W.C.

Sep 25. 52 '92

Dear Mr Stevenson

I wonder if you can
quite realise the joy with
which I heard that the "little
Minister" had passed muster in
ye household at Samoa. As for
the earl, I never brought him
on (you will see from my
phraseology this I am writing for the
stage) without first kicking him
round the room. I told Meredith
your criticism of the end, and he
(daresay) agreed with it. I never
[saw] L[or] a chapter in the

Barrie

1892 *Letter to Robert Louis Stevenson*

J. M. BARRIE WAS ELATED upon receiving a letter from his longtime idol, the writer Robert Louis Stevenson, in the summer of 1892. Stevenson informed Barrie that he was not only aware of Barrie's work, but that he enjoyed it immensely. Indeed, in a letter to Henry James that same year, Stevenson wrote that "you [James] and Barrie and Kipling are now my Muses Three."[1]

Barrie replied to the news that *The Little Minister* had reached Stevenson by explaining his methods for writing, then continued with comments on Thomas Hardy—noting that, in *Tess of the d'Urbervilles,* "The Dairymaids seemed to me to be comic opera figures"— and on Rudyard Kipling and Arthur Quiller Couch: "He is writing a novel with 274 leading characters."

The two Scotsmen (and fellow alumni of Edinburgh University) continued a detailed correspondence until Stevenson's death on December 3, 1894. Barrie's dream of visiting him in Samoa was sadly unrealized, but he memorialized his friend in the poem, "Scotland's Lament."

1. Letter to Henry James, December 5, 1892, in *The Letters of Robert Louis Stevenson*, ed. Bradford A. Booth and Ernest Mehew (New Haven: Yale University Press, 1994–95) vol. 7, p. 450.

THE ROMANCE THAT THE THEATER OFFERED J. M. Barrie had human faces in the actresses who became his favorites and inspired his writing. One ingénue who had a particularly strong effect on Barrie was Mary Ansell, who was introduced to him by the humorist Jerome K. Jerome. After their first meeting, Barrie promised her a leading role in *Walker, London,* produced in 1892.

Following an extended and, by all appearances, chaste courtship, the couple wed on July 9, 1894. Mary Barrie retired from the stage but soon had to cope with her husband's increasing focus on his work and on the Llewelyn Davies children. Their marriage would last until 1909.

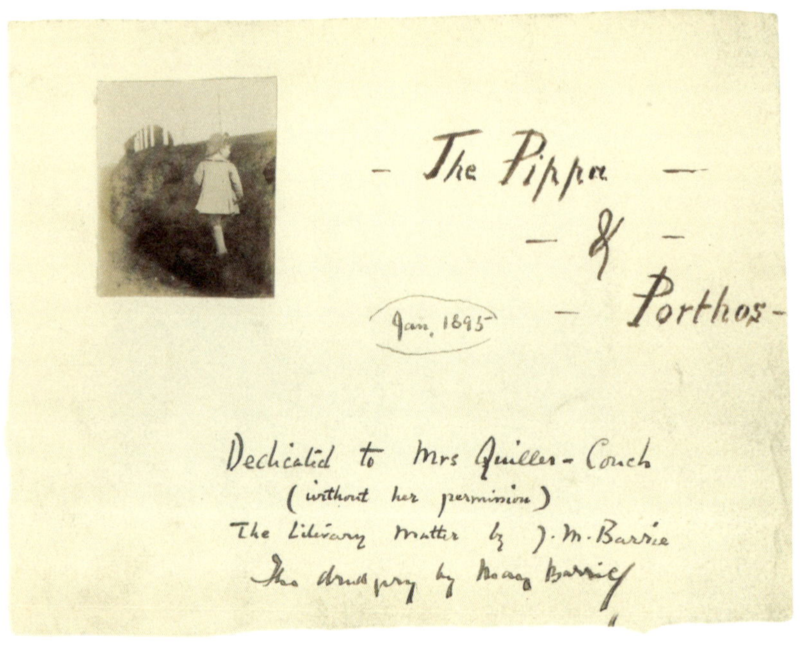

Dedicated to Mrs Quiller - Couch
(without her permission)
The Literary matter by J. M. Barrie
The drapery by Maggy Barrie

"Why have you stopped?" asked the Pippa.
"Because you look so dashed cocky," replied Porthos.

1895 *Page from* THE PIPPA AND PORTHOS

J. M. BARRIE'S DEDICATION TO CHILDREN, or more broadly to the idea of childhood, can be seen as one of the most intense themes of his life and his work. Though he paid close attention to his own nephews and nieces, he doted on the children of close friends who were often in his company.

Arthur Quiller Couch, best known as "Q," the author of fantastic and supernatural tales, was the father of Bevil, whom Barrie nicknamed "The Pippa." Barrie took a series of snapshots of Bevil playing with the Barries' St. Bernard, Porthos, and composed a picture book to record the friendship of the little boy and the patient dog. Porthos would star in another unique Barrie production six years later, *The Boy Castaways of Black Lake Island.*

92.

And now I am left without them, but I trust my memory will ever go back to those happy days, not to rush thro' them, but dallying here and there, even as my mother wanders thro' my books. And if I also live to a time when age must dim my mind and the past comes sweeping back like the shades of night over the bare road of the present, it will not, I believe, be my youth I shall see but hers, not a boy hanging to his mother's skirt and crying, "Wait till I'm a man, and you'll lie on feathers" but a little girl in a magenta frock and a white pinafore, who comes toward me thro' the long parks, singing to herself, and carrying her father's dinner in a flagon.

"The End
Aug 11. '56

CA. 1895 *J. M. Barrie and his mother*

1896 *Draft page of* MARGARET OGILVY

PERHAPS THE GREATEST TRIBUTE an author can make to a mother is to write her biography. Barrie doted on his mother, Margaret Ogilvy (who retained her maiden name in observance of local Scottish custom), and made sure she did not want for anything as long as he could provide for her. Her death at age 76 in 1895 had a palling effect on Barrie. Though she could always be found in the background of his Auld Licht stories, Barrie resolved to dedicate the preface of his novel *Sentimental Tommy* to her. This preface eventually grew to book length. *Margaret Ogilvy,* published in December 1896, purports to recount episodes in the life of J. M. Barrie's mother, but as he figures in most of the anecdotes, it also serves as an autobiographical work.

1896 *Artwork for* SENTIMENTAL TOMMY

SENTIMENTAL TOMMY WAS a more fully realized extension of Barrie's fictionalized childhood. This is the tale of the childhood of Tommy Sandys, destined to become an orphan, whose "sentimentality" toward others is so overwhelming that he lives in a world detached from reality. The publication of the novel serially in *Scribner's* magazine in 1896 firmly established Barrie with the publishing firm in the United States.

The illustrations by W. L. Hatherell include this scene near the end of the story in which Grizel (whom Tommy will eventually marry in the sequel, *Tommy and Grizel*) is found watching over the body of her mother, "the Painted Lady," who has succumbed to consumption.

RESULT OF THE TEST MATCH, 1898.

1899 *Illustration from* THE ALLAHAKBARRIE BOOK OF BROADWAY CRICKET

From early boyhood, J. M. Barrie was a fan and player of cricket. In 1887, he recruited a number of his fellow writers to form a league to play games during summer holidays. In the 18 seasons that the team gathered, players included, among many others, Arthur Conan Doyle, A. E. W. Mason, and P. G. Wodehouse. The team's name was a combination of the Arabic exclamation for "Heaven Help Us" and the name of the team founder. Broadway was a small village in Worcestershire popular with English and American artists.

In 1899, Barrie and his teammates put together a booklet detailing rules and successes of the team. The illustration here depicts Barrie with the honorary captain of an opposing team, Mary de Navarro, the former stage actress Mary Anderson.

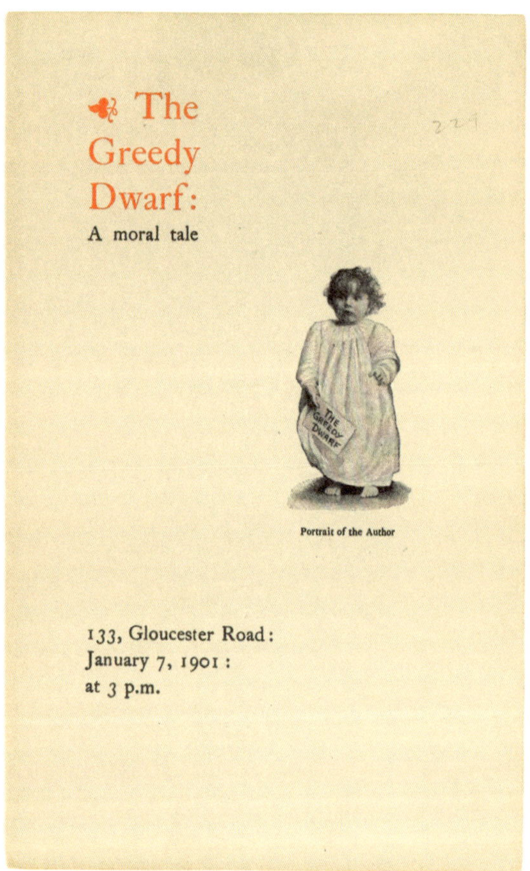

The Greedy Dwarf:

A moral tale

Portrait of the Author

133, Gloucester Road:
January 7, 1901:
at 3 p.m.

The Allahakbarrie Cricket Club

Has the Honour to present

for the first and only time on any stage

an Entirely Amazing Moral Tale

entitled

The Greedy Dwarf

BY PETER PERKIN

Prince Robin Miss Sylvia du Maurier

Sleepyhead . . .	Mr. Mason
Cowardy Custard .	Mr. Barrie
Allahakbarrie . .	Mr. Gerald du Maurier
Bruin, a Bear . .	Mr. Bright
Policeman . . .	Mr. Meredith
Chang, a Dog . .	Mr. Porthos
Dame Trot . .	Miss Priscilla Prunes

AND

Brownie . . Miss Mary Contrairy

SCENE I.	A Glade in the Forest
SCENE II.	The Same Glade in Another Forest
SCENE III.	The little Schoolhouse in the Wood
SCENE IV.	The Horrible Home of the Greedy Dwarf

Chief of the Orchestra . . Mrs. Meredith

Enormous Engagement of

Miss Sylvia du Maurier

Who has been Brought Back from the
year 1892 in a Hansom to play

The Principled Boy

Have you never seen Mr. Bright as a Bear?
No? Then you have never seen him at Home

The School Scene
will contain

A Scathing Exposure
of
Our Educational System

Miss Mary Contrairy
will spell *Allahakbarrie* in
the last Act

The whole
to conclude
in

A Blaze of Glory

1901 *Program for* THE GREEDY DWARF

Dᴜʀɪɴɢ ᴀ ᴡᴀʟᴋ ɪɴ ᴋᴇɴsɪɴɢᴛᴏɴ ɢᴀʀᴅᴇɴs in the latter part of 1897, J. M. Barrie encountered a group of boys being tended by their nurse. The two oldest of these gregarious children struck up a friendship with the author and his dog. On New Year's Eve of that year, Barrie found himself sitting next to a beautiful creature named Sylvia, who was soon revealed to be the mother of his newest friends. The Llewelyn Davies family had now formally entered his life.

Barrie showed his devotion to the family by making up stories for the boys, and he wrote the play *The Greedy Dwarf* as a private entertainment. It was performed in the Barries' drawing room with Barrie playing the villain, "Cowardy Custard," who menaces "Brownie," played by his wife Mary. The true hero of the play was Porthos, their dog, who was enticed to wrestle the villain to the ground in a fit of excitement, bringing cheers from the audience, children of Barrie's friends.

xxv. They had to sit outside, because their brother was within singing, and playing on a barbaric instrument. 'The music,' said Peter, 'is rude, and to a cultivated ear discordant; but the songs, like those of the Arab, are full of poetic imagery.'

1901 *Cover and page from* THE BOY CASTAWAYS OF BLACK LAKE ISLAND

IN 1900 THE BARRIES BEGAN to spend summers in a small cottage in Surrey in the south of England. The following year, the Llewelyn Davies family summered in a nearby village, which meant that Barrie could see George, Jack, Peter, and baby Michael every day. Remembering his joy in making *The Pippa and Porthos,* Barrie set out to create a much more extravagant narrative starring the boys. Based on a mixture of themes, adventure stories, pirate legends, and the children's own games, Barrie assembled *The Boy Castaways of Black Lake Island,* in which Porthos again played a supporting role.

In the 1928 preface to *Peter Pan,* Barrie would reflect that in *The Boy Castaways of Black Lake Island* were the origins of much of the play. Of the two copies Barrie had made, only the one in Beinecke Library survives, making it a unique volume in Barrie's bibliography.

XIV. Peter Pan.

If you ask your mother whether she knew about Peter Pan when she was a little girl she will say 'Why, of course I did, child,' and if you ask her whether he rode on a goat in those days she will say 'What a foolish question to ask; certainly he did.' Then if you ask your grandmother whether she knew about Peter Pan when she was a little girl she also says 'Why of course I did, child,' but if you ask her whether he rode on a goat in those days she says she never heard of his having a goat. Perhaps she has forgotten, just as she sometimes forgets your name and calls you Mildred, which is your mother's name. Still she could hardly forget such an important thing as the goat. Therefore there was no goat when your grandmother was a little girl. This shows that in telling the story of Peter Pan, to begin with the goat (as most people do) is as silly as to put on your jacket before your vest.

Of course it also shows that Peter is ever so old, but he is really always the same age, so that does not matter in the least. His age is one week, and though he was born so long ago he has never had a birthday, nor is there the slightest chance of his ever having one. The reason is that he escaped from being a human when he was seven days old; he escaped by the window and flew back to the Kensington Gardens.

If you think he was the only baby who ever wanted to escape,

it shows how completely you have forgotten your own young days. When David heard this story first he was quite certain that he had never tried to escape, but I told him to think back hard, pressing his hands to his temples, and when he had done this hard, and even harder, he distinctly remembered a youthful desire to return to the tree tops, and with that memory came others, as that he had lain in bed planning to escape as soon as his mother was asleep and how she had once caught him half way up the chimney. All children could have such recollections if they would press their hands hard to their temples, for having been birds before they were human they are naturally a little wild during the first few weeks and very itchy at the shoulders where their wings used to be. So David tells me. [I ought to mention here that the following is our way with a story. First I tell it to him and then he tells it to me, the understanding being that it is quite a different story, and then I retell it with his additions, and so we go on until no one could say whether it is more his story or mine. In this story of Peter Pan, for instance, the bald narrative and most of the moral reflections are mine, though not all, for this boy can be a stern moralist; but the interesting bits about the ways and customs of babies in the bird-stage are mostly reminiscences of David's, recalled by pressing his hands to his temples and thinking hard.

Well, Peter Pan got out by the window, which had no bars. Standing on the ledge he could see trees far away, which were doubtless the Kensington Gardens, and the moment he saw them he entirely forgot that he was now a little boy in a nightgown, and away he flew, right over the houses to the gardens. It is wonderful that he could fly without wings, but the place itched tremendously, and perhaps we could all fly if we were as dead confident—sure of our capacity to do it as was bold Peter Pan that evening.

He alighted gaily on the open sward between the Baby's Palace and the Serpentine, and the first thing he did was to lie on his back and kick. He was quite unaware already that he had ever been human, and thought he was a bird, even in appearance, just the same as before, and when he tried

BARRIE'S FRIENDSHIP WITH the Llewelyn Davies family had a significant effect on his writing as well as on his personal life. He reflected on his walks in Kensington Gardens by making notes for a new kind of book—one in the format of a conversation between an older narrator and a young boy. This idea evolved into a collection of stories concerning landmarks in Kensington Gardens. Barrie had begun to invent stories of this type to entertain George, Jack, and Peter in which boundary markers became stones for dead children buried by a willful baby boy who had escaped his nursery and now cavorted with fairies.

The birth of Peter Pan, who was formally introduced in 1902 in chapter 14 of *The Little White Bird,* signaled a new focus for Barrie. He began to address the fantasies of a new generation of children, just as he was putting to rest the last sentimental account of his own childhood in *Tommy and Grizel,* the last chapter of his Auld Licht tales, which was also published in 1902, to a less-than-enthusiastic response from his readers.

children because they
recognise the truth
of them

2) Children sh'd be
real children with
central interest —
but nothing difficult
to do

3) Ellaline their mother ?
or Lena Ashwell —
or Mrs Campbell .
or Ellen Terry .

4) Cd ghost "mother"
(L as B) work
into this ?

5) Peter "Mother, how
did we get to
know you ?"

2/6
J. M. Barrie

Leinster Corner
.
Lancaster Gate .

London W.

oct   1902

1) Fairies

important character
the mother treated
(from child's point
of view — how mother
scolds, wheedles &c
scenes in which
children's behaviour
to her and which

6) Irving's boy "was
like a new 'Crockery'
competition on "Crichton"

7) The "Joey" chapter

8) of off eleven

8) Michael dancing
at Wrtlings chapel
& bell tolling

funeral of another
child

9) Duke of York
appearances (small
character)
"Super" If I ad have
a play written
round me."
Brand Bring them
all in
Porcupine bent on the

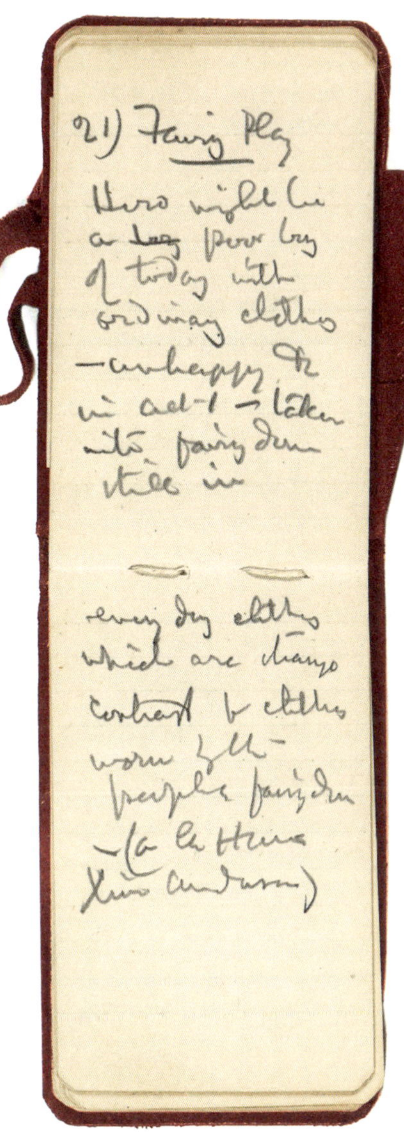

FAIRY TALES WERE A STAPLE of Victorian children's reading. Indeed, the vogue of fairy lore, in stories and in paintings by the likes of Richard Dadd, having evolved from ancient legends and supported by writers such as Shakespeare, had a hold on the 19th-century English imagination. Andrew Lang's 12-volume Fairy book series (beginning with the *Blue Fairy Book* in 1889) codified the old and modern tales for a wide audience. It was a natural extension, then, for fairy plays to find an appreciative juvenile and adult audience.

For Christmas in 1901, Barrie took the oldest Llewelyn Davies boys to a production of *Bluebell in Fairyland,* a runaway success aimed at children. Barrie was so impressed by the play that he engaged the lead actors, Ellaline Terriss and Seymour Hicks, for his next play, but the greater impact gestated a bit longer as Barrie began making notes in his pocket notepad for his own fairy play.

THE DASHING VALENTINE BROWN [MR. S. HICKS].

MISS TERRISS, MISS MARION TERRY AND MISS FILIPPI.
"PATTY BRINGS AN EXTRA CUP FOR A FOLLOWER."

1902 QUALITY STREET *souvenir postcards*

QUALITY STREET is the tale of two sisters, one of whom, Phoebe Throssel, pulls off a deception on her suitor, Valentine Brown, who must leave to fight in the Napoleonic wars. When he returns, Phoebe passes herself off as her "niece" Livvy, a vivacious flirt. When Valentine declares his love for Livvy, Phoebe reveals herself and wins her lover for her true self.

The genteel whimsy of this drama proved quite successful during its London run in 1902. Ellaline Terriss and Seymour Hicks, the real-life couple who starred in this production, were known to Barrie from their earlier play, *Bluebell in Fairyland*.

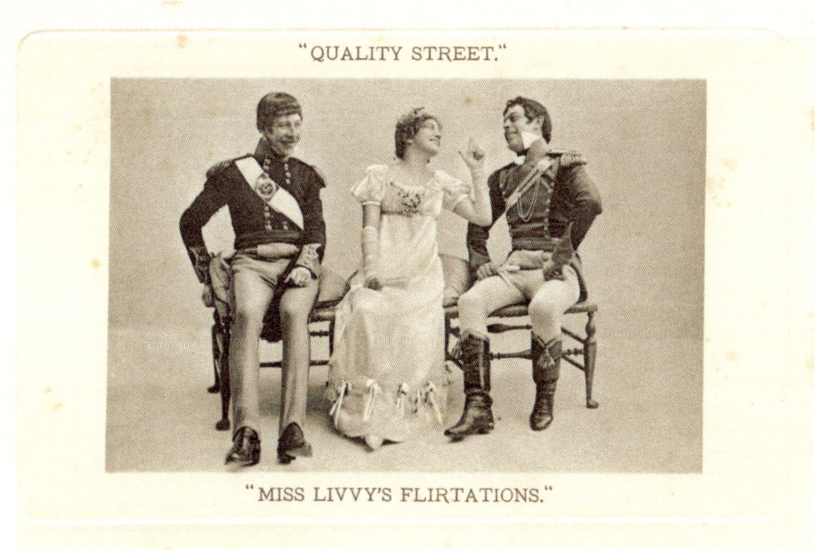

1902 THE ADMIRABLE CRICHTON

Photograph of 1914 stage production

THE ADMIRABLE CRICHTON was written in parallel with *Quality Street* in the early days of the 20th century. The play was produced on the London stage and ran concurrently with *Quality Street* during the 1902–1903 theater season. Far from being a light piece of farce, *The Admirable Crichton,* though likely to be classed as a comedy, explored much deeper social themes.

The play centers around a titled family that is shipwrecked along with their servants on a desert island. Roles are quickly reversed as a new social hierarchy is established— one based on survival skills—in which the butler rules the island. By the end of the play, the castaways are rescued and back in London, where order has been restored. In early versions of the play, there is no argument against this restored order, but, in later revisions, Barrie injected speeches in which Crichton, the butler, rejects his return to servitude. The play has been filmed a number of times, including a 1919 Cecil B. DeMille adaptation, *Male and Female.*

The title of the play derives from the legendary 16th-century Scottish prodigy, James Crichton, a symbol of the ideal man. This scene, on the desert island, dates from a production possibly from 1914.

23) Chauvau[?] lines "Will not be a _____" &c
24) Chauvau Harlequin thing – Peter origin of Harlequin[?]
25) In Cinderella ballet of Peter & Fay &c – similar to in [illegible] scene
26) Peter a rebel agst mothers – admirts[?] affections but hymns[?], like any g. independence – [illegible] liked g. things &c
27) Alphabetical biscuits[?] &c
28) Peter in [illegible] – get trifter[?] horror g. matrimony
29) Peter [illegible] on parents g. ordinary children – [illegible] games &c – stole time – [illegible] g. sleeping in [illegible] &c
30) Peter says nothing really means anything – [illegible] & stops middle g. sal [illegible] says &c – just[?] "[illegible]" mustn't think
31) He is agst parents "[illegible] made g. think"
32) How about Peter his effect g. making all people feel "like children" Parents &c –
33) 'Thus some father (Kunll[?]) or schoolmaster in harlequinade
34) Peter in air with things attached to adults' scenes to be [illegible] their dance [illegible] g. wild [illegible] [illegible]
35) Peter might be about child g. thus [illegible] – [illegible] that he flies away.
36) [illegible] to father abt babies "Rather" sweets, [illegible] he joking[?] & (touching)
37) Father kind to say love [illegible] there &c
38) Dog licking
39) Peter might show both children g. how to dance.
40) Fun in old Peter womb[?]
41) Till boy dog dies & is [illegible] in bed – tool[?] ([illegible])
    both fairies person [illegible] [illegible] fairies & (trapped[?])
42) children having – dreams [illegible] to give the servants
43) [illegible] sing about – ill end they guests who fly in to life in to dinner[?]
44) Musical-taking morning girl g. clothes   42-3 – 18-8 &c
45) an explosive [illegible] reminds but fires him like buttons eggs a "cool"
46) Fly funny but in right measure.
47) Infanti[?] people or always in a prison.
48) Swing dog medicine
49) Prince kicks [illegible], she says thanks g. this is a great day for me Delight g. prince when him kicks back.
50) Prince won't [illegible]
51) Cupids [illegible] arrows into prince
52) Prince g. beauty competition
52) Child – "are you bigger than favour?" (or adept)
53) Probably the whole g. children [illegible] g. off on adventures

54) To boy princes it would be romantic & [illegible] but be among poor g. see their pleasures, all usual to him – they leave &c mind – & make believe – it is all done for him
55) Striking price g. children universe & detachment their [illegible] in crim places (scaffolds &) funeral.
56) Thy might – [illegible] into sea to save dog.
57) He might be turned into a boy in [illegible] – their rescued.
58) Taking children off to battle them
59) Dramatic audience g. Peter window – night – & [illegible] – [illegible] ordinary way – dog [illegible] – Peter [illegible] on [illegible]
60) Peter angry at their being other children – wanted mother to [illegible] – had meant to thy – went now – [illegible] in telling them
61) Dog licking from water jug
62) Dog commissioned g. mother to keep them always in bed – he dances as usual like a nurse.
63) Window always kept open g. mother g. their to fly back &c
64) Peter's shadow [illegible] before he appears – dog sees & [illegible] [illegible] g. original – but abt eating or cutting off shadow[?] (parents examine shadow &c) is it [illegible] too (keep shadow like photograph) Peter [illegible] at it & head to hand to [illegible] & [illegible] a clock.
65) Girl like angels.
66) In [illegible] thy have up &c came [illegible] anything wanted to – boy anything it is [illegible] to him.
67) Child – [illegible] [illegible] – their boy to [illegible] – to all girl dog new.
68) The songs g. any are "father g. [illegible] &c really said g. crime [illegible] dull in [illegible] with ghost – & beg [illegible] paid for – but might to children really – Right – [illegible]
69) Marriage g. children – Peter would attend in black (and g. [illegible])
70) Dancing at funeral g. child might be [illegible] round bed – heartface & finest morning (bell tolling)
71) Fly might be founded on ghost – mother in [illegible] – the arms g. watching children at night. He examines clothing, sees, puts in order – scenes femin fire – children [illegible] but [illegible] mustn't pretend [illegible] – added mother knows she's dead. g. [illegible] thinks she is a prisoner somewhere.
72) If so that old man, her son – thy [illegible] – and that he he says will [illegible] with her – & [illegible], – when it always she is gone, he is sitting dead.

1903 *Note for the play* ANON

WHILE BARRIE WAS ENJOYING new heights of success with two of his plays, *Quality Street* and *The Admirable Crichton,* running concurrently to full houses, he found himself deeply focused on his newest project. This fairy play, with the working title of *Anon,* built on the story of the lost boy he had conjured in *The Little White Bird.*

His detailed notes from October 1903 show his imposition of rules on the fantasy world of the play, his detailed philosophy for creating a complete theoretical universe for Peter Pan governed by such principles as:

"19—Peter is a sprite, inveigling children away from becoming grown up"

"28—Peter in love but [?] horror of intimacy"

"[40]—Fun is all Peter wants"

Tiger-Lily
Eagle feathers

Peter Pan.

1904 *Costume designs for first production of* PETER PAN

CHARLES FROHMAN, Barrie's American producer, was enchanted by the story of Peter Pan and set about to organize a spectacular production, engaging the best players and inventing technologically sophisticated apparatuses to allow actors to fly on stage. The matter of costumes and set design was delegated to William Nicholson, one of England's most respected portraitists, who painted Barrie in the spring of 1904. Nicholson, also known for his exemplary woodcuts, imagined the cast of characters drawn from Barrie's ideas, but fitted out with an artist's eye.

Peter emerged as the amalgam of his favorite haunts, with one hat made of feathers, the other of dried grass. Tiger Lily was outfitted in a broad mix of American Indian costume elements, including feathers, porcupine quills, and strings of wampum beads. The pirates hewed to the standard loose stereotype, with Starkey even sporting an eye patch made of sailcloth. Before the play opened, the Peter Pan costume was completed by Henry J. Ford.

Poisoned. Nonsense! Who could have poisoned it. I
promised Wendy to take it and I'm going to as soon as I've
sharpened my dagger.

(He is sharpening it on a revolving
grindstone, TINK darts to glass and
is seen apparently drinking it, but the poison merely
goes down stem)

Now then! Tink, you've drunk my medicine.

(TINK darts about strangely)

What's the matter with you?

(Bells)

It was poison! You drank it to save my life. Tink
dear Tink, are you dying.

(TINK flies into her little room and to bed
rings feebly)

She's dying. (to audience) Her light's growing faint,
and if it goes out, that means she's dead. Her voice
is so low I can scarcely tell what she's saying.

(Weak bells - he runs between her and audience)

She says she thinks she could get well again if
children believed in fairies. Do you believe? Say quick
that you believe! If you believe, clap your hands, clap
clap.

(The light has been flickering, but now children
in audience are expected to begin to demonstrate)

Wave your handkerchiefs so that she may see you believe. Don't let Tink die. The light's getting stronger
wave, wave, wave. She's much better - she's all right now
Oh, thank you, thank you   And now to rescue Wendy!

(He puts a mask over his face, rushes upstairs
and off L. looking for track. TINK darts about

1904 *Page from production script of* PETER PAN

As the debut of peter pan grew near at the end of 1904, technical details had to be worked through. The presence of Tinker Bell (who had been named, at one stage, Tippy Toe) was a matter for the lighting and sound crew, as it had been decided that she would appear as an energetic flash of light reflected off carefully placed mirrors, accompanied by a vocabulary of bells and rings.

This page from the production script shows the sequence of cues that followed along with one of the most gripping moments in the play—when Tinker Bell drinks the poison that Captain Hook has planted for Peter. It is Peter's appeal to the audience to clap their hands to save her that has become a classic scene of modern staging.

ALFRED ELLIS
& WALERY
COPYRIGHT
51, BAKER STREET
LONDON, W

1905 *Nina Boucicault as Peter Pan*

THE ROLE OF PETER PAN ON STAGE would be a difficult proposition for any actor. Barrie wanted a young boy to play the role, but eventually agreed with the idea of having a young woman play him, in line with the Victorian pantomime tradition. In addition, labor laws imposed restrictions on children under the age of 14, so several of the other male roles, including most of the Lost Boys, went also to female players.

The choice for Peter was at arm's length. Dion Boucicault, Jr., the director, suggested his sister Nina, who delighted audiences as well as critics. (Sadly, she played the role for only the first season.) Gerald du Maurier, the uncle of the Llewelyn Davies boys, played Captain Hook as well as Mr. Darling. Hilda Trevelyan originated the part of Wendy, a role she reprised for several seasons and tours.

Duke of York's Theatre,

ST. MARTIN'S LANE, W.C.

Proprietors	Mr. & Mrs. Frank Wyatt.
Sole Lessee and Manager	CHARLES FROHMAN

EVERY AFTERNOON at 2.30, and EVERY EVENING at 8.30,

CHARLES FROHMAN

PRESENTS

"PETER PAN,"

OR

THE BOY WHO WOULDN'T GROW UP.

A Play in Three Acts, by

J. M. BARRIE.

Peter Pan ...		Miss NINA BOUCICAULT
Mr. Darling		Mr. GERALD du MAURIER
Mrs. Darling		Miss DOROTHEA BAIRD
Wendy Moira Angela Darling		Miss HILDA TREVELYAN
John Napoleon Darling		Master GEORGE HERSEE
Michael Nicholas Darling		Miss WINIFRED GEOGHEGAN
Nana ...		Mr. ARTHUR LUPINO
Tinker Bell		Miss JANE WREN
Tootles		Miss JOAN BURNETT
Nibs		Miss CHRISTINE SILVER
Slightly		Mr. A. W. BASKCOMB
Curly	(Members of Peter's Band)	Miss ALICE DUBARRY
1st Twin		Miss PAULINE CHASE
2nd Twin		Miss PHYLLIS BEADON
Jas. Hook	(The Pirate Captain)	Mr. GERALD du MAURIER
Smee		Mr. GEORGE SHELTON
Gentleman Starkey		Mr. SYDNEY HARCOURT
Cookson		Mr. CHARLES TREVOR
Cecco	(Pirates)	Mr. FREDERICK ANNERLEY
Mullins		Mr. HUBERT WILLIS
Jukes		Mr. JAMES ENGLISH
Noodler		Mr. JOHN KELT
Great Big Little Panther		Mr. PHILIP DARWIN
Tiger Lily	(Redskins)	Miss MIRIAM NESBITT
Lisa	(Author of the Play)	Miss ELA Q. MAY

Beautiful Mothers, Redskins, Pirates, Crocodile, Eagle, Ostrich, Pack of Wolves, by Misses Mary Mayfren, Victoria Addison, Irene Rooke, Gladys Stewart, Kitty Malone, Marie Park, Elsa Sinclair, Christine Lawrence, Mary Maddison, Gladys Carrington, Laura Barradell, Daisy Murch. Messrs. E. Kirby, S. Spencer, G. Malvern, J. Grahame. Masters S. Grata, A. Ganker, D. Ducrow, C. Lawton, W. Scott, G. Henson, R. Franks, E. Marini, P. Gicardo, A. Biserga.

ACT I.—OUR EARLY DAYS. Inside the House. (Mr. W. Harford.) **ACT II.—THE NEVER, NEVER, NEVER LAND.** Scene 1.—The House we built for Wendy. (Mr. W. Hann.) The Curtain will be lowered for a few moments. Scene 2.—The Redskins' Camp. (Mr. W. Hann.) Scene 3.—Our Home under the Ground.	**ACT III.—WE RETURN TO OUR DISTRACTED MOTHERS.** Scene 1.—The Pirate Ship. (Mr. W. Harford.) Scene 2.—A last glimpse of the Redskins. Scene 3.—How to know your Mother. Scene 4.—Outside the House. Scene 5.—The Tree Tops. (Mr. W. Hann.)

The Play produced under the Direction of Mr. DION BOUCICAULT.

General Manager ... ... (For CHARLES FROHMAN)	W. LESTOCQ

The Esquimaux, Pirates and Indian Costumes designed by Mr. W. NICHOLSON, and executed by Messrs. B. J. SIMMONS, 7, King Street, Covent Garden. Miss Boucicault's Dress designed by Mr. HENRY J. FORD. Miss Baird's Costumes by Madame HAYWARD &, New Bond St. Miss Trevelyan's Dresses designed and executed by SHEBA, 17, Sloane Street. The Beautiful Mothers' Dresses designed and executed by Madame J. BLANCQUAERT & Co., 38 & 39, South Molton Street. The Dances invented and arranged by Mr. W. WARDE. The Music composed and arranged by Mr. JOHN CROOK. The Flying Machines supplied and worked by Mr. G. KIRBY. Properties supplied by Mr. LOUIS LABHART, 18, Queen's Square, W.C. Stage Mechanist, Mr. H. THOMPSON. Electrician, Mr. C. HAMBLETON. Property Master, Mr. W. BURDICK.

Stage Manager	DUNCAN McRAE	Musical Director	JOHN CROOK
Business Manager		JAMES W. MATHEWS

Extract from the Rules made by the Lord Chamberlain

(1.) The name of the actual and responsible Manager of the Theatre must be printed on every play bill. (2.) The Public can leave the Theatre at the end of the performance by all exit and entrance doors, which must open outwards. (3.) The fire-proof screen to the proscenium opening will be lowered at least once during every performance to ensure its being in proper working order. (4.) Smoking is not permitted in the Auditorium. (5.) All gangways, passages and staircases must be kept free from chairs or any other obstructions, whether permanent or temporary.

S. HAMMERSMITH & CO., PRINTERS, 49, FLORAL STREET, COVENT GARDEN.

1905 *Satin program for* PETER PAN

BY ALL ACCOUNTS, *Peter Pan* was a success. It premiered at the Duke of York's Theatre on December 27, 1904, to a (mainly adult) audience. This odd mixture of fantasy, pantomime, and audience interaction won them over from the first scene, in which Nana prepares Michael for his bath. The play was praised by critics and ran for 12 performances weekly until April 1st of the following year.

An American production, starring Maude Adams, opened in New York in November 1905 to equally enthusiastic response. Back in London, a revival was mounted for the 1905–1906 season. *Peter Pan* was presented in London every year since its premiere until it was interrupted by the war in 1939.

HOOK ACT III.

PETER AND WENDY ACT I.

ACT. III.

ACT. II. & V. Scene I.

CA. 1905 *Peter Pan toy theater*

THE SUCCESS OF *Peter Pan* spurred a deluge of associated products—books, toys, souvenirs—whether they were officially licensed or not. Public demand for *Peter Pan* memorabilia brought the production of such items as a *Peter Pan* card game, posters based on scenes from the play, and postcards of favorite actors.

One of the most elaborate keepsakes was a *Peter Pan* toy theater. The Victorian vogue for toy theaters—miniature, usually colored, printed sheets that reproduced characters and sets from well-known plays—had all but passed by the time of *Peter Pan*. While older toy theaters were made from engravings, the set for *Peter Pan* was produced from photographs taken of the first London production. 

With each piece cut out and mounted to a support, children could act out the entire play or invent their own adventures. This rare survivor came from the family of Arthur Quiller Couch, Barrie's good friend, "Q."

MICHAEL.

A POEM

LEINSTER CORNER,
LANCASTER GATE, W.
7 Jan 1906.

A⁵ any Asses that don't love my Mick,
B⁵ what I fling at them, namely a Brick,
C⁵ Combinations, with Michael inside,
D⁵ Normandy Davies, where he once did reside.
E⁵ Evian water, his favourite drink,
7 is his Friend, who is that, do you think?
G stands for George, his elder brother,
H for 14 and 2, that alarmed mother.
I stands for Imp, which applies to the lot o' you,
J is for Jack who is sometimes too hot for you.
K is the Kids who don't do as you wish,
L the eel caught at Davies when we went out to fish.
M your dear Mary, who's always awake,
N Nick, who's your sweet mother's smallest mistake,
O the Oil you are told for to take like a man,
P stands for Peter and Peter for Pan.
Q are the Questions Mick asks for to pose me,
R my Replies, which are vain he knows me.
S stands for Sylvia, Mick's delight,
T is his Tu'penny when tucked in at night.
U is U silly who are reading this letter,
V is your Vanity, you couldn't do better,
W old Willie, who is still bouncing boys,
X is the Xs sent Mick with his toys,
Y is the Yawns I give till we meet,
Z are the Zanies who are not at his feet.
                                    J. M. B.

1906 MICHAEL / A POEM

OF THE FIVE LEWELYN DAVIES BOYS, it has often been observed that Barrie was most deeply devoted to Michael, possibly because he was the first brother whom Barrie knew from the moment of his birth. This poem, composed for Michael when he was 5½ years old, contains many references that are either obscurely personal or dated. One question has an obvious answer: "F is for Friend, who is that, do you think?"

Some people can smoke to excess.
Let them beware. There are
others can't smoke to excess because
there isn't time enough in a day which
contains only 24 hours. But never
mind about that: the matter which
touches me much nearer, is the
question, who got this book from poor
Edward & Charles?

Guess it.

Mark Twain

To J. M. Barrie.

August/08.

Transferred to
Michael Llewellyn Davies
by the afore-mentioned
J. M. Barrie
June 16 1910

Edward and Charles Sisson

San Francisco

March 12, 1885

1908/1910 *Inscribed copy of* THE ADVENTURES OF HUCKLEBERRY FINN

ONE OF BARRIE'S MANY ADMIRERS was Mark Twain, creator of Tom Sawyer and Huck Finn. Twain wrote to Maude Adams, star of the American production of *Peter Pan,* that the play was ". . .a great refining and uplifting benefaction to this sordid and money mad age. . ." [1]

In 1908, Twain made a gift to Barrie of a copy of *Huck Finn*—in a curious fashion. The copy he sent appeared to be one that had been sent to Twain for an autograph, but that Twain forgot to return. He did the original owners, apparently the Sisson brothers of San Francisco, the favor of including them in his dedication. Barrie passed the book on to Michael Llewelyn Davies two years later.

1. Phyllis Robbins, *Maude Adams: An Intimate Portrait* (New York: Putnam, 1956), p. 90.

1912 *J. M. B. and Michael Llewelyn Davies*

A FORMAL PORTRAIT FROM 1912 shows Barrie and Michael outfitted for fishing.
As the brothers got older, they grew fond of fishing excursions with Barrie to Scotland.
By the time of this photograph, Barrie had taken formal custody of the boys following
the deaths of their parents—Arthur in 1907 and Sylvia in 1910. Barrie, now a bachelor
again, looked after the boys with the assistance of a staff and a separate residence for
them. He saw to their education, with most of the boys attending Eton, Captain James
Hook's alma mater.

At six t'was thus I wrote my name,

> J Barrie,

At twelve it was not quite the same,

> James M. Barrie

At twenty thus, with a caress,

> James Matthew Barrie,

At thirty I admired it less,

> J. M. Barrie,

At forty-fifty it was so,

> J. M. B.

And soon I think the _m_ will go,

> J. B.

One tear for twenty's youthful swank,
And then the name becomes a blank.

CA. 1913 *Verse in copy of* QUALITY STREET

SOMETIME AROUND 1913, Barrie inscribed a limited illustrated edition of his play, *Quality Street,* for an unidentified dedicatee. This bit of simple rhyme tells much more than it seems. The evident expansion, then contraction of his name exhibits the usual lament of growing old, but for Barrie, the physical act of writing was itself a major concern as he grew older. At the age of 59, in 1919, he developed a debilitating cramp in his right hand. He taught himself to use his left hand — again, since he had favored it as a young boy — and found that his handwriting was remarkably legible.

This inscription is from the period before he made the switch. The last two lines, which show the deteriorating quality of his penmanship read:

One tear for twenty's youthful swank,
And then the name becomes a blank.

Mar 5. 1917

My dear Mary,

It would be silly of us not to meet, and indeed I wanted to go to you all day yesterday. I thought perhaps you would rather come here, and of course whichever you prefer is what I would prefer, but that is your only option as I mean to see you whether the idea scares you or not. Painful in a way the first time but surely it need not — be so afterwards. How about

1917 *Letter to Mary Cannan*

FOLLOWING HIS DIVORCE IN 1909, Barrie devoted himself to his work and to the care of his new wards, the Llewelyn Davies boys. Though he was not one to provoke much speculation on romantic matters, he continued his fascination with beautiful actresses, including Gaby Deslys, for whom he fashioned the failed ragtime revue, *Rosy Rapture, or the pride of the Beauty Chorus.*

His former wife Mary who eventually married Gilbert Cannan, the man who precipitated her divorce from Barrie, in turn divorced Cannan as well. Upon hearing this news, Barrie sent a sympathy note to Mary beginning: "It would be silly for us not to meet . . ." Indeed, Barrie retained an affection for Mary throughout his life, and even though Mary had made veiled critiques of her ex-husband in her own books, Barrie made provisions in his will to provide her with an annuity after his death.

Evenings, 8:20.   Matinees Wednesday and Saturday, 2:20.

CHARLES FROHMAN
PRESENTS

WILLIAM GILLETTE

—IN—

DEAR BRUTUS

A COMEDY IN THREE ACTS

BY

J. M. BARRIE

The fault, dear Brutus, is not in our stars,
But in ourselves, that we are underlings.
—Shakespeare

Characters in Acts I. and III.

MR. DEARTH .... WILLIAM GILLETTE
MRS. DEARTH .... HILDA SPONG
MR. PURDIE.............................REX McDOUGALL
MRS. PURDIE .... MYRTLE TANNEHILL
MR. COADE .... GRANT STEWART
MRS. COADE .... MARIE WAINWRIGHT
LOB .... J. H. BREWER
MATEY .... LOUIS CALVERT
JOANNA TROUT .... ELISABETH RISDON
LADY CAROLINE LANCY..........VIOLET KEMBLE COOPER

Characters in the Wood

THE ARTIST ....MR. DEARTH
MARGARET, his daughter.....................HELEN HAYES
THE HON. MRS. FINCH-FALLOWES............MRS. DEARTH
THE PHILANDERER .... MR. PURDIE
JOANNA, his wife.....................JOANNA TROUT
MABEL .... MRS. PURDIE
THE PIPER .... MR. COADE
JAMES MATEY .... MATEY
CAROLINY, his wife.......................LADY CAROLINE

SYNOPSIS OF SCENES

ACT I.—LOB'S HOUSE.

ACT II.—THE WOOD.

ACT III.—SAME AS ACT I.

Produced under the stage direction of Iden Payne.
Stage Manager, Edward Broadley.
Scenery by Homer Emens.
Ladies dresses by Henri Bendel, Inc., and H. Milgrim & Bros., Inc.

1917 *Playbill for* DEAR BRUTUS

THE EVENTS OF THE WAR YEARS led Barrie to write on more serious themes. Two of his best-reviewed plays premiered in 1917. *The Old Lady Shows her Medals,* a one-act, was a forceful if eccentric reaction to the war. The plot concerns a woman speaking to friends about the letters (her "medals") she receives from her son, who is off fighting in the war. At the end of the play, it is revealed that she has no son and all of the letters are blank sheets of paper.

In *Dear Brutus,* a group of partygoers enters a magic forest that offers them all a second chance to make important choices in their lives. Though the title is taken from *Julius Caesar,* the fantastic mix of melancholy and metamorphosis is more closely aligned with *A Midsummer Night's Dream.* Though he had perished two years earlier, Charles Frohman is listed as the producer for this American production—because there were many projects in the works at the time of his death.

No. 1815.] THURSDAY, JUNE 15, 1922. [Price 3d.

In memory of Michael Llewelyn Davies, Editor of the *E.C.C.* in 1918, these two sonnets, which he wrote at Eilean Chona, an island on the west coast of Scotland, in August 1920, are given here with the approval of his guardian. Michael would have been twenty-two to-morrow.

EILEAN CHONA.

I.

Throned on a cliff serene Man saw the sun
hold a red torch above the farthest seas,
and the fierce island pinnacles put on
in his defence their sombre panoplies ;
Foremost the white mists eddied, trailed and spun
like seekers, emulous to clasp his knees,
till all the ~~beauty~~ of the scene seemed one,
led by the secret whispers of the breeze.

The sun's torch suddenly flashed upon his face
and died ; and he sat content in subject night
and dreamed of an old dead foe that had sought and found him ;
a beast stirred boldly in his resting-place ;
and the cold came ; Man rose to his master-height,
shivered and turned away ; but the mists were round him.

II.

Island of sleep, where wreathèd Time delays,
haven of things remote, indulgent, free,
Thou whose encircling mists in autumn days
veiled the intruder on thy secrecy ;
he there beheld bright flowers in a dream
join with tall trees to cheat the Cyprian,
and heard in murmurs of a woodland stream
Arcadian measures of resurgent Pan ;

Yet will not tread again thy perfumed shore
and mount the coloured slope beneath the trees,
or there release his senses ever more
to tread the footprints of old deities,
so thou do not send echoes to remind
of those sweet pipes, and charm him from his kind.

ταῦτα μνήμῃ κεχαρίσθω.

1922 ETON COLLEGE CHRONICLE

THE YEARS OF THE FIRST WORLD WAR and the first years of the 1920s were difficult for J. M. Barrie. He had five quickly maturing young men to watch over, as well as his own professional reputation on the stage. The war affected every English family. Barrie felt the first wave of devastation in March of 1915 when the news reached him of the death of George Llewelyn Davies on the Western Front in Flanders. Two months later, Barrie's  longtime producer and friend, Charles Frohman, drowned when the *Lusitania,* on which he was traveling to England, was torpedoed by a German U-boat.

The most devastating blow came after the end of the war. Michael Llewelyn Davies, who had intended to enlist in the British Army on November 12, 1918, was one day too late to serve. Fate, instead, sent him to Oxford. It was there, on May 19, 1921, that he and a companion were drowned in a dangerous swimming hole.

One year after his death, the *Eton College Chronicle* published his verses memorializing visits to his favorite Scottish island where he had spent many happy hours with Barrie.

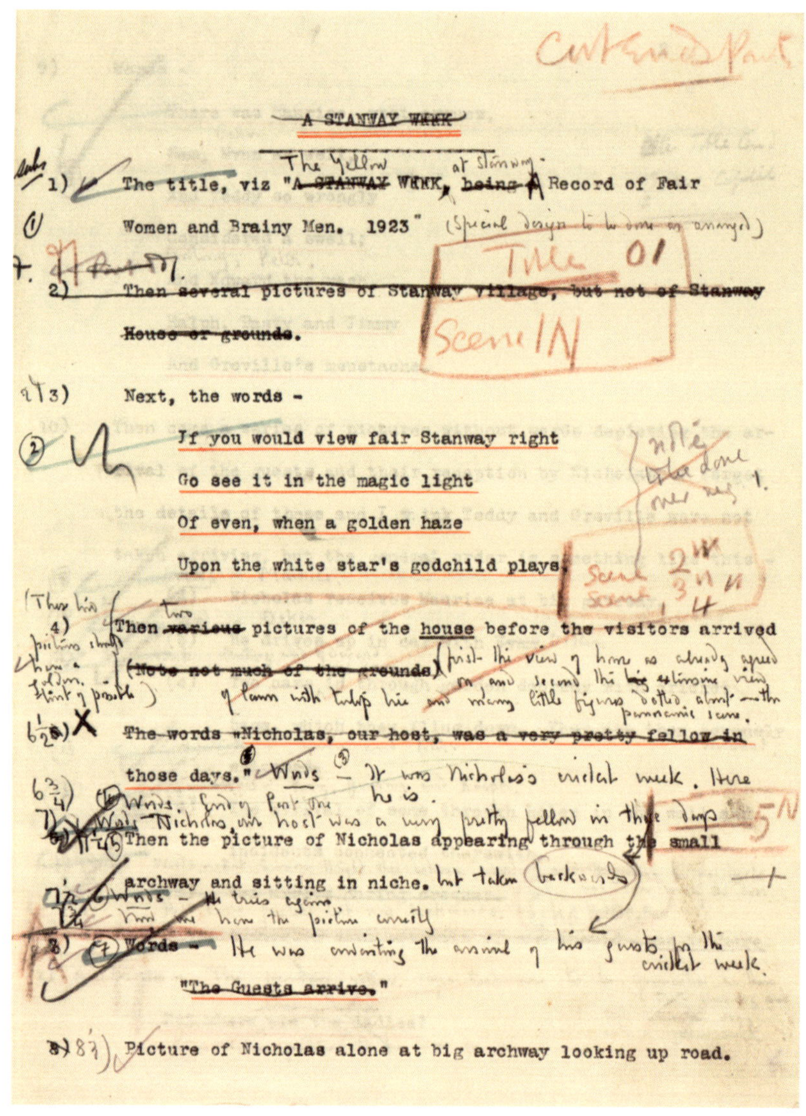

A STANWAY ~~WEEK~~

1) The title, viz "A ~~STANWAY WEEK, being~~ A Record of Fair

Women and Brainy Men. 1923"

2) ~~Then several pictures of Stanway village, but not of Stanway~~

~~House or grounds.~~

3) Next, the words –

If you would view fair Stanway right

Go see it in the magic light

Of even, when a golden haze

Upon the white star's godchild plays.

4) Then ~~various~~ pictures of the house before the visitors arrived

~~(Note not much of the grounds)~~

5) ~~The words «Nicholas, our host, was a very pretty fellow in~~

~~those days."~~

6) Then the picture of Nicholas appearing through the small

archway and sitting in niche.

7) Words –

"The Guests arrive."

8) Picture of Nicholas alone at big archway looking up road.

1923 A STANWAY WEEK *script*

IN THE SPRING OF 1921, Barrie spent the first of many long vacations at Stanway, the country house of his friends, Lord and Lady Wemyss. This spacious estate in the Cotswolds became a gathering place for many of Barrie's friends when he began renting the house during his summer holidays. In 1922, he entertained Queen Mary at the house.

In subsequent years, Barrie started a tradition of producing a play every summer featuring his guests. His original works included such plays as *Tomorrow and Tomorrow and Tomorrow* and *Where is Simon, or The Secret of the Pyramid*. The first of these works was actually a film script, eventually titled *The Yellow Week at Stanway —A Record of Fair Women and Brainy Men*. The page shown here features Nico Llewelyn Davies as a main character. It was at Stanway that Nico met his future wife, Mary James, daughter of Lord Northbourne.

J. M. Barrie
3 Adelphi Terrace House
W. C

To the Five.

Some disquieting confessions must be made in printing at last the play of Peter Pan, among them this, that I have no recollection of having written it. Of that, however, anon. What I want to do first is to give Peter to the Five without whom he never would have existed. I hope, my dear sirs, that you will accept this dedication with your friend's love; and indeed, as all the other plays of mine that I care to print are included in this same volume, I beg you, in memory of what we have been to each other, to allow me to throw in the lot. The play of Peter is streaky with you still, though none may see this save you and I. A hundred acts had to be left out, and you were in them all. We first brought Peter down, didn't we, with a blunt-headed arrow in Kensington Gardens? I seem to recall that we believed we had killed him, though he was only winded, and that after a spasm of exultation in our prowess the more soft-hearted among us wept and all of us thought of the police. Once upon a time there was not one of you who would not have sworn as an eye-witness to this occurrence; no doubt I was abetting, but you used to provide corroborative evidence that was never given to you by me. As for myself, I suppose I always knew that I made Peter by rubbing the five of you violently together, as savages with two sticks produce a flame. I am sometimes asked who and what Peter is, but that is all he is, the spark I got from you.

What spent we had of him until we clipped him small to make him fit the boards. He was the longest story on earth, and some of you were not born when it began and yet were highly finished before we all saw

1928 *Manuscript of* TO THE FIVE

Dᴇsᴘɪᴛᴇ ᴘᴇᴛᴇʀ ᴘᴀɴ's ɢʀᴇᴀᴛ ᴘᴏᴘᴜʟᴀʀɪᴛʏ, the text of the play was not published until 1928. Barrie had responded to the demands of his fans by expanding the Peter Pan chapters from *The Little White Bird* into the book *Peter Pan in Kensington Gardens* in 1906, followed by *Peter and Wendy,* in 1911. When the stage version of *Peter Pan* was finally offered to the public as part of a uniform edition of his plays, Barrie had revised the text at points and added lengthy production notes (including the notice that Peter was never to be touched by any other character).

The most significant addition, though, was the dedication "To the Five," the five being the boys who had inspired the play. Barrie had created the play from a jumble of fairy tales, childhood obsessions, pirate stories, and personally invented myths, but he ascribed the origin of the play to the Llewelyn Davies brothers:

I suppose I always knew that I made Peter by rubbing the five of you violently together, as savages with two sticks produce a flame. I am sometimes asked who and what Peter is, but that is all he is, the spark I got from you.

Sᴛ JAMES'S PALACE,
S. W. I.

April 18th, 1929.

Dear Sir James,

      As President of the Great Ormond Street Hospital, I write to thank you most sincerely for having presented to the Hospital all your rights in 'Peter Pan'.

      I cannot think of a more appropriate gift to help sick children and, together with all those who have the interests of the Hospital at heart, I am very grateful to you for your happy thought.

      Believe me,

      Yours very truly,

Edward P

Sir James Barrie, Bt., O.M.,
  3 Adelphi Terrace,
    W.C.2.

1929 *Letter from Edward, Prince of Wales*

By the time the text of peter pan was published, the play had become a seasonal favorite in England and in America. It was also providing Barrie with a comfortable income. The year following the publication, in what seemed a surprising move to many of his friends, Barrie assigned the copyright to *Peter Pan* to the Great Ormond Street Hospital in London. This generous act provided the hospital with a continual source of operating funds. Edward, Prince of Wales, personally wrote to Barrie to express his gratitude.

The copyright for *Peter Pan,* which was to have expired in 1987, was extended that year in perpetuity by the Prime Minister of England.

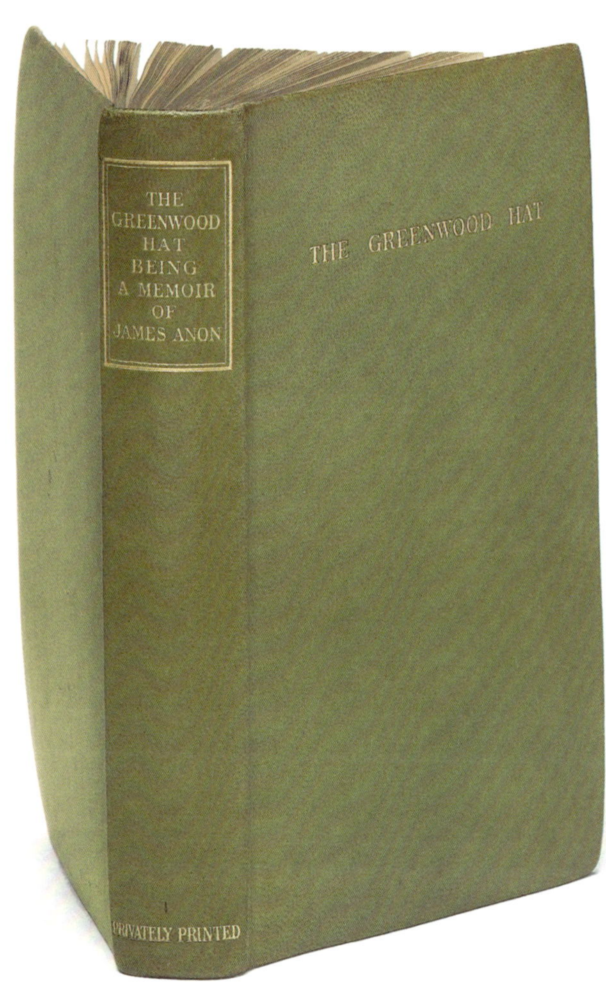

THE
GREENWOOD
HAT
BEING
A MEMOIR
OF
JAMES ANON
THE GREENWOOD HAT
PRIVATELY PRINTED

1930 THE GREENWOOD HAT

THOUGH BARRIE NEVER ISSUED a public memoir or full autobiography, he did write about his life in a limited edition book (of 50 copies) distributed to his close friends and family in 1930: *The Greenwood Hat,* named for Barrie's historic meeting with the editor of the *St. James's Gazette* in 1885. The book is attributed to "James Anon," a pseudonym that combines Barrie's given name with an earlier nom-de-plume (*Anon,* also the original title of *Peter Pan*).

Barrie introduces the book as being "merely some old newspaper articles tied together with a string of memories." In evaluating his early work, Barrie states: "He was a humble atom was Mr. Anon, but I am glad he worked so hard."

Peter Llewelyn Davies published a more widely distributed edition in 1937, following Barrie's death.

Goliath scene

(Ophir casts the horn into the glade)

Abner   Know, boy, that there is none in the
         land who will face this ~~man~~ monster.
Voices   None — none.
Abner   He is as one left over from the giants
         who were drowned in a deluge and now
         ~~mourn and groan~~ groan in Hell beneath the
         waters. Such is this Goliath who
         cometh here to our dishonour, crying
         mockingly that Israel is without a
         God.
David   Who is the god of Israel?
Abner   Our maker, whom Goliath defies.
Jonathan Touch not the horn, David. Surely
         now you are afraid
Ophir   Ah see how Samuel's champion trembles.
         In vain do we ~~await~~ await the
         blast that was to be great in
         Israel.
David   Perhaps I am afraid — but
         thus does David.
         (He lifts the horn and blows, &c
         ~~&c~~ (The answer comes from Philistine
Goliath armour-bearer (appearing) Goliath
         awaits the champion of Israel in
         the Vale of Elch" indicating that it lies
         where he has come from. Other
         business as before.
A Slinger A darkness comes upon the

1937 *Goliath scene from* THE BOY DAVID

IN THE 1930s, James Matthew Barrie had entered his seventh decade. His plays were being widely produced, and films were adapted from several of them with varying degrees of success. Barrie could have easily slipped into a noble retirement. Instead, he once more developed an infatuation, one that led to his last great work. This time, he fell for the Austrian-born actress Elisabeth Bergner, who had caused sensations in Germany and in France. When Barrie saw her in London in *Escape Me Never* in 1934, he resolved to write a play for her talents.

Together, they agreed to work on a far-reaching biblical theme—the story of David and Goliath. After a period of starts and stops, Barrie's *The Boy David,* with Miss Bergner in the title role, opened in London in December 1936. Audiences did not respond enthusiastically and this final major work, which had occupied the last years of Barrie's life, ended a short run in late January 1937. The scene shown here is a late revision to the end of the play, where David confronts the Giant.

Whereas

This Indenture

made this 10th day of June One thousand nine hundred and thirty seven Between James Matthew Barrie so called Author and Her Royal Highness the Princess Margaret

Witnesseth as follows:

Whereas the above mentioned hence forward to be called the said Barrie did write and otherwise indite a play of short and inglorious life called "The Boy David" and basely produce the aforesaid play as exclusively the work of his own hand

And whereas some of the play including all the best of it namely two lovely sentences admired by all readers who have read the English version in the Scottish tongue was immediately and penetratingly and excitedly recognized by the aforesaid Her Royal Highness the Princess Margaret as emanating not from the artful James Matthew Barrie above mentioned but from a far superior brain (namely her own) and according to all dictionaries the Princess is therefore his collaborator she demands her legal share in all his monetary rights and royalties in said play and the other revenues rentals perquisites and emoluments that are well known to roll in one continuous and golden stream from dramatic undertakings

And whereas the said Barrie did imply and implicate when thus challenged that he knew of collaborators who could not even spell the word (meaning Her Royal Highness Princess Margaret) and that he had never collaborated with anyone

And whereas Her Royal Highness promptly replied that there were people called Policemen who were friends of hers and she would ask the biggest of them to smash and wholly destroy the so called Barrie unless he paid up immediately

Whereupon this Barrie was so cowed that his face became wet with tears and terrors

1937 *Indenture between J. M. Barrie and Princess Margaret*

THOUGH THE BOY DAVID was neither a critical nor a commercial success, it did prove a worthwhile project for Barrie. He wrote out of devotion to his leading lady, and he was able to show that his imaginative powers had not waned completely.

One true fan of the play was young Princess Margaret, who reminded Barrie that she was, in fact, a co-author of the play. During a summer visit, she had spoken of Barrie: "He is my greatest friend, and I am his greatest friend." It did not go unnoticed by the princess that Barrie had incorporated this line, and one other she had spoken, into the script for *The Boy David.* A solution to the uncredited appropriation was decided upon. A royal indenture was drawn up to guarantee an overdue payment to Barrie's collaborator of one penny for every time her lines had been spoken on stage. Barrie gathered 170 new pennies, but died nine days after signing the indenture, before he could deliver them.

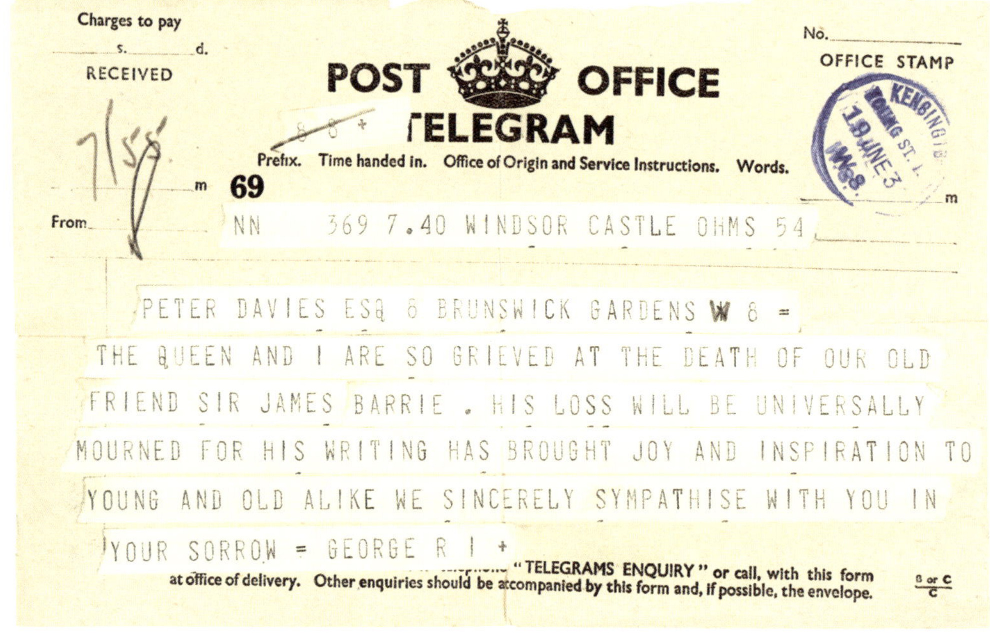

Charges to pay
s.   d.
RECEIVED
No.
OFFICE STAMP
POST OFFICE TELEGRAM
Prefix.   Time handed in.   Office of Origin and Service Instructions.   Words.
m 69
From
NN   369 7.40 WINDSOR CASTLE OHMS 54
PETER DAVIES ESQ 6 BRUNSWICK GARDENS W 8 =
THE QUEEN AND I ARE SO GRIEVED AT THE DEATH OF OUR OLD
FRIEND SIR JAMES BARRIE . HIS LOSS WILL BE UNIVERSALLY
MOURNED FOR HIS WRITING HAS BROUGHT JOY AND INSPIRATION TO
YOUNG AND OLD ALIKE WE SINCERELY SYMPATHISE WITH YOU IN
YOUR SORROW = GEORGE R I +
at office of delivery.   Other enquiries should be accompanied by this form and, if possible, the envelope.
"TELEGRAMS ENQUIRY" or call, with this form

1937 *Condolence telegram from the King of England*

THE NEWS OF BARRIE'S DEATH, at the age of 77, on June 19, 1937 had a profound effect on his many fans in the United Kingdom and around the world. Barrie, a Scotsman, had become emblematic as the chronicler of British small-town life in the late Victorian era and the storyteller for the youth of the Edwardian era.

The royal family expressed condolences in a telegram to Peter Llewelyn Davies, now an established publisher, yet still a man who would always be associated with his famous namesake.

ACKNOWLEDGMENTS

Mᴀɴʏ ᴘᴇʀsᴏɴs ᴀssɪsᴛᴇᴅ in many ways with the creation of this exhibition and catalogue. Christa Sammons, Harold Dozier and Patrick Kiley offered editorial assistance and research. The majority of the images used in this catalogue were prepared by the staff of the Beinecke Digital Library project: Ellen Cordes, David Driscoll, Christopher Edwards, Andrew Hungaski, Rebekah Irwin, Ann Marie Menta, and Matthew Shirley. Event coordination progressed smoothly because of the work of members of Beinecke's administrative staff: Kathy DiMaio, Jennifer Kniesch, Rebecca Martz, Doreen Powers, and Regina Romero. Frank Turner, director of the Beinecke Library offered guidance and encouragement, as did many other staff members of the library, all of whom dedicate their talents to our collections, exhibitions, and events on a daily basis. Catherine Waters, whose skillful hand can be seen in all aspects of the design of these catalogues, all of the printed items created for the exhibition, and the exhibition itself, was an imaginative colleague during the months-long process to reach our goals. Very importantly, a few extremely patient people helped at all stages of this project by providing support, good humor, and immeasurable doses of much-appreciated advice: Andrew Birkin, John Hill, Nancy Kuhl, and Kathy Martinson.

LIBRARY OF CONGRESS CATALOGING-IN-PUBLICATION DATA

Young, Timothy G. (Timothy Garrett), 1965–
    My heart in company : the work of J.M. Barrie and the birth of Peter
Pan / Timothy Young.
        p. cm.
    A companion catalog for the exhibition "My heart in company : the work
of J.M. Barrie and the birth of Peter Pan," held at the Beinecke Rare
Book and Manuscript Library, Feb. 3 – Apr. 23, 2005.
   ISBN 0-8457-3159-9
  1. Barrie, J. M. (James Matthew), 1860–1937—Bibliography—Exhibitions.
2. Barrie, J. M. (James Matthew), 1860–1937. Peter
Pan—Bibliography—Exhibitions. 3. Barrie, J. M. (James Matthew),
1860–1937—Characters—Peter Pan—Bibliography—Exhibitions. 4. Peter
Pan (Fictitious character)—Bibliography—Exhibitions. 5. Children's
stories, English—Bibliography—Exhibitions. 6. Fantasy fiction,
English—Bibliography—Exhibitions. 7. Boys in
literature—Bibliography—Exhibitions. I. Beinecke Rare Book and
Manuscript Library. II. Title.

  Z8076.Y68 2005
  [PR4076]
  016.828'91209—dc22
                      2004028928

COLOPHON

Published January 2005
by Beinecke Rare Book and Manuscript Library
Yale University, New Haven, Connecticut
in an edition of 3,000

Design and typography: Catherine Waters
Prepress supervision: Joseph Maynard, Publishing Services Center
Color and print consultation: Sue Medlicott
Printer's negatives: John Robinson, and the staff at Gist and Herlin Press
Printing: Gist and Herlin Press
Foil stamping: Lehman Brothers
Binding: Efficiency Bindery

Items pictured on pages 28, 58 and 59 are the gift of Frederick R. Koch.